Phoenix

A Memoir of Mental Illness

by Nikita Wing

Phoenix A Memoir of Mental Illness

Published in the United States of America

Camden, Maine

Published   by Inked Toad Press, Camden, Maine, USA

Dedicated to my mother who always tells me
the truth and shows me how important truth is
in this world. She's a beautiful Earth Angel.
I thank God for her every day,

Chapter One   Earth Angels Among Us

There's something to be said about an earth angel. In my opinion, you know when you meet them. They are here to spread love, trust, and encouragement. Just by knowing them, they make your whole world a better place to live. I believe my mother and my aunt are both earth angels. Everything they say and do spreads love and kindness to you. You know most times when you meet an Earth Angel. Just being around them makes your day brighter. Some may say who did that? I had a dark cloud hovering over me for the past 6 months and I'm happy now, I'm smiling. I feel good. It may have been an encounter with an Earth Angel.

When I was a child, I remember getting hurt on the monkey bars. I fell off, I got a scrape on my wrist. I was 7 years old. Someone told my mother and she came running, swooped me up, held me then cleaned out the sore. At that moment I knew I had the best mother and the best fit for a mother for me.

I've had a rough life; however, I have had two amazing parents. My whole family is amazing. I could not ask for a better family. I love them, dearly. They are all wonderful people. I do have a mental illness. I was diagnosed at fourteen years old with bipolar disorder with psychotic features. I was young and felt like this death sentence hovered over me. I was young and couldn't put into words what was happening to me. All I knew was to act out. Yell, scream, punch, get angry, call others names, and try to hurt people. And I did hurt people.

I hurt my mother. My mother was trying to help me. All I knew was to fight. I didn't understand why she was dropping me off at St Mary's Psychiatric Unit in the adolescent ward. Only my mother seemed to know what a long hard obstacle I would face ahead of me.

It has been long, hard and painful. Yet mental illness is a breathtakingly beautiful ride. The world shakes within you with each articulate thought. What a beautiful ride. What a blessing it is to be alive. I don't always feel that way, most days I want to curl up in a ball and hide from the world. Pretend that I don't exist even just for a second. Depression sinks in and I need to get away in another place in my mind. Usually, I think of a life much better than mine and I fantasize about being in that life. I get lost in it. It makes me smile. Then reality sinks in. I'm not there in that fantasy. I'm back on planet earth. I've been living underneath this cloud of utter pure darkness. To this day as I write this book, I still feel this way. A sense of peace comes over me when I think about my angels and spirit guides and how I know they are there protecting me, loving me, and being there for me. I hope.

My angels have made their presence known many times. They are there with me. Not only can I feel them, but there was also a point in time when I was 16 years old, I was looking up angels online and I felt this sense of peace come over me. I was all alone in my house. I said *hi* -to my angels- *can you give me a sign you are here with me right now?* I had my hair up in a ponytail and the next thing I knew my ponytail was being tugged on. I smiled and said I knew they were here and there is life after death. My aunt Cindy is one of these beautiful Earth Angels. She is dying of cancer right now. We are all very sad. My mom and my aunt are as close as two people can be. She's beautiful in God's eyes and the world's eyes. She's truly blessed. Anyone that knows her is blessed for being in the presence of this angel, I wish my mom knew more than she does that my aunt Cindy will be all right there when she passes. I think my mom just needs time to process. I like to think that when we die this physical body dies but we do not die. We go home to heaven, everything is energy. Our physical bodies keep us here on earth.

I've had other experiences where other things have happened. I guess through my mental illness I found peace and closure from so many things. I had to say goodbye to people through my spirituality. It filled a space in me that needed to be filled. There was a place in me where it needed to be filled... my self-worth.

I have had a really hard life. I was sexually abused at 6 years. After that everything became chaotic. my mom and dad were split up. My mom was doing the right things. My dad was doing the right thing. But they both wanted custody of me. So, my dad would take me away from my mom and my mom would to court to fight for us back. Finally, my mom had permanent custody. I think that they were both amazing parents that loved me so much. They both wanted to care for me until the day I left home to make sure I was alright. As I sit here writing, tears come to my eyes because I still have a hard time - thinking of myself as a victim, not a survivor. I have to say to myself - *whoa I survived that I'm not a victim anymore.* The victim road in my storybook is beaten up, torn to shreds, whereas the survivor path is immaculate. I guess I better start thinking of myself as a survivor too.

In my life, I've heard and seen things. I've been delusional, psychotic. I've been depressed. I've gone through the ups and downs. I've gotten knocked back down and gotten back up. I refuse to let this illness win. I keep thinking to myself and asking God, "How many times do I have to get knocked back down before I can get up and stay up for good?" Maybe I felt sorry for myself one too many times. I was feeling sorry for myself, but I had that right to feel that way, didn't I? I had the right to hide away from the world for periods so I did. To this day I still hide away from the world every once in a while. I isolate myself to protect my heart. I'm reminded during those times that life can be peaceful too. When I can meditate on the good going on in my life and I can discard the bad. It leaves me feeling refreshed and attuned with what I'm doing on this earth.

Even as I write this, I say to my higher power *why am I here?* It is okay to question that. I was fourteen when I was hospitalized for the first time. The bars on the windows told me it wasn't a safe place to be and I wanted to leave. It was foreign to me. People were being restrained. People were screaming. I hated it there.

Then after many hospitalizations in St. Mary's Hospital, I went to the Brattleboro Retreat in Vermont and it couldn't have been a better fit for me. I was well behaved so they moved me to t 4 the unit for people who behave. I felt like I had poured my heart and soul out to my counselors there and I did. Not only did they give me a nudge in the right direction for my future they saved my life. I'm positive I would have committed suicide. I am forever grateful for them, for my life. I'd like to think it is what was written. In my blueprint. Before we come to earth, we write our own lives. I strongly believe in that. I like the way that feels too. Because I have nobody to blame but myself. I'd rather not be angry at somebody else. So, for some reason, I'd like to think I chose my life. I wrote it in my chart. And I like to think life is like school and we come here to learn for God. I hope I can bring back everything God needs to learn.

Sometimes I start screaming inside. No! Why! I don't want to get up, I don't want mornings, I don't want to move, I don't want to think I don't want to do anything... I am big on having one look on my face and then feeling a wreck on the inside. But I chose to come here for a reason. Whatever that reason is, I have no clue why I'd hope it would be to help people. That would make every ounce of pain I've felt worth it even just to help one person. I've gone through a lot in my life.

I have a schizoaffective disorder which is similar to paranoid schizophrenia. I think it's safe to say I've had over 20 psychotic breaks in my life so far. And I am just 33 years old. When I say, "I have demons head-on," I mean I have faced them head-on and then some. I remember back in 2008 I had a psychotic break, my partner at the time and I were not doing well and I was delusional and my partner left and took the cats and I had this eerie feeling come over me. I kept throwing up. I am not sure to this day if it was an overdose or not. I had begun to hear and see things. I would have called somebody for help but I had no clue during that time what a phone was. Other psychotic breaks I've had, I've known how to use phones. One time I started running up the middle of a very busy street. People were calling 911. I was running in the middle of it. The police came. I was close to getting tasered had I not gotten into the ambulance. It's difficult to be in a position to take care of yourself when you do not even know who you are. You don't remember your past, your future, things that made sense to you before are non-existent in a world full of delusions. You are living in a dream world lost in terror fear and the undeniable truth that at that moment there's no way out. However, for me, there was this little voice in my head saying "Are you sure you want to be running up the middle of that busy road? Are you sure you're okay, why not go to the hospital?" Then once I'd snap out of those moments of hell and terror (psychotic breaks) I'd be fine again and look in the mirror and know that I was truly the only one in this whole world who knew how bad I had it. I could say it describes it, but it terrified me to the core to know that I was living something that nobody else in the whole world had experienced too. And that terrified me. That nobody really knew.

 I've probably had over 20 psychotic breaks in my life. I went from being a popular cheerleader in high school to someone who dropped out and went into a psych ward after psych ward to later going to a long-term treatment facility in Vermont. Sometimes the truth hurts. I had a therapist at the retreat that was a hard therapist. I guess she wanted me to be all set when life gets too hard for me. My life had completely changed within months from high school to the psych ward. I used to be outgoing now. I'm introverted. Getting kicked in the ass by a mental disorder not only brought me down to reality a million notches but it opened my heart to what life truly has to offer. How good things could get better or worse depending on our thoughts. How we have the power to change our thoughts and feel better because everything is ultimately in our control.

I love writing by the ocean.

Chapter 2   Meditation Over Hearing Voices

I like writing about the waves and how they come crashing down and how it cleanses us from inside out. I'm grateful for those times and feel blessed. One time when I was having a psychotic episode, I grabbed the car keys and it was in the middle of winter at around 1 a.m. I was hearing voices. I drove around the lake in Auburn about seven times going about 60 miles per hour.   The roads were all icy and then the voices started saying "Go to Walmart." So I did. I went to Walmart and went shopping. When I got to the register, I must have not swiped my card in the right way and it was declined. I left my cart there and just left. I drove back home and was having delusions that my roommate had killed himself and I was walking into a crime scene. The thing about being psychotic is that you smell everything - it traumatizes you.

 I have struggled more than you could imagine but the rest of my book will NOT be about my struggles, it will be about having faith, showing love, having trust, believing in yourself. Anything and everything spiritual. I don't want this book to be about doom and gloom. I'm writing this to tell you you're worth it. I'm worth it. I am a survivor of so many things and so are you.

When I was 22 years old, I overdosed on medication and I was delusional for about 6 months after. I got sent to a hospital, dropped my bags at the door, and yelled, " I'M HOME NOW!" Of course, the nurses and people working there thought it was funny, they started laughing. While I was there, I had no concept of time. I don't even know if I was eating. I wasn't showering. I was having back-to-back delusional episodes. While I was there, I ended up believing that one of the staff was trying to hurt me so I ended up assaulting her and 3 other staff members. I honestly had no clue what I was doing. I got a deferred disposition because I never had a criminal record before and I was very sick. After that incident, they kicked me out to go home. I had no idea where my home was - being delusional and everything. Once we were close by, the taxi driver dropped me off and I went with what looked familiar to me. I broke open the door to my apartment with my shoulder.

That night was the scariest night of my life. I was having delusions that I was being watched through my windows by my old partner's parents and I sat there on my couch and every little sound sounded like them cutting the screen to my kitchen window open it with a knife and then I heard a gun and they started talking to me in my ear saying "Don't make one move!" They had all their guns and knives out and they had stapled black trash bags over every inch of my apartment and were planning on killing me. There would be no evidence after. So, I stayed sitting up all night in fear. What I learned from this is so deep and is myself. I found myself. It revealed that I had never taken good care of myself. All of that because I was not taking the appropriate steps to take good care of myself.

I'll make a vow as long as you do to take good care of ourselves. It is terrifying the effects it can take on your body, heart, mind and soul to not take care of yourself. I've never really done drugs or drank alcohol. Except for when I was a young adult once or twice. I would have much rather found my high meditating by the beach listening to music than taking the headphones off and listening to the waves coming crashing down. We are all blessed. We live in a world full of beauty. Mother nature is everything. I find that in times when I'm most in need of a hug or love or comfort I talk to Archangel Raphael because I've been told he's around me often. And on those hard nights when I feel like giving up, I ask him why I'm still here on this earth. I get angry at him. But then I feel this overwhelming comfort and the answer becomes clearer than ever, I'll leave this earth when it is my time to. I've had to face many psychotic breaks in my life. Sadly, they wouldn't stop so I had to hospitalize myself and put myself in a group home. I've had breaks when I was living in my car and saw my ex-partner sitting in the back seat eyes glowing red like he was a demon. I've also had delusions when I saw him standing next to the wall in the kitchen and he put a gun to his head and blew his head off. Delusions can be happy, terrifying or sad. They can be anything. I remember nights when I'd stay up all night laughing with the voices in my head.

Mental illness is, however, a beautiful thing in my eyes; you see life through a whole new set of lenses. Things that you've overlooked before are beautiful in my eyes. I have now, this want and nagging feeling to help, mental illness may be an invisible disease, where you can't see it but so many can feel it. I've always tried to hold myself together. I figured I would hide it and try to keep myself together on the outside to not show how bad it was on the inside.

I've struggled since I was 14 years old. I was a cheerleader and had a lot of friends. And as freshman year was ending, I started staying in bed a lot. I left high school. My friends noticed how depressed I was and they ditched me. I found true friends later down the road. I learned that I held in too much and did not say anything to anyone. Please if you're struggling say something, don't hold it in. Mental illness is something that can be positive. It's a beauty in disguise. Just the way, I look at the whole world now. Yeah, I may have those times when I pray to my angels to let me die. I ask them how much longer I have. I got my answer. It's not my time to go. Because I'm still a living, breathing being in the world. Then at times, I get angry at them. I get the same answer again. Getting angry will not solve the problem. I'm here for a reason. I think I don't want to be here for a reason.

But I am. I guess my angels win those conversations. Honestly, I just want to be here to help people. That would be all that I could ever ask for.

I remember this one time I overdosed on a heavy medication and

Chapter 3   Psychotic Breaks

I had an appointment with my doctor at the time that day. It was clear to anyone that laid their eyes on me how sick I was. After my appointment, the evening was coming and I started screaming things outside and to the guard. I was screaming at the guard to shoot me. They had to escort my doctor out to her car in fear that I might hurt her. Then the police came and put me in the backseat of the cop car. He asked me what my name was and I gave him like 3 or 4 different names. Then I gave him my real name. When I gave him the different names, I wasn't chosen I was confused as to who I was.

I know times seem difficult now but things do get better. I believe the earth is like school. Our physical bodies are here to hold us down in this world but we are so much more than our physical bodies. We are energy. We are mind, body, heart, soul and spirit. And I believe we come here to grow, learn, teach. I believe we write out our lives before we come here and come to hell or high water, we must finish our destiny. Sometimes I close my eyes and wonder what it would be like to not be sick anymore. I've gone from hospital to hospital feeling sicker each time. I wonder what it's like to be normal again. Back when I was happy. I used to find moments in my childhood where I'd look around and say I'll remember this moment for the rest of my life. This moment is perfect. Nothing was going wrong, everything was going right. I didn't expect my life to turn into psych wards, psychotic breaks, and group homes but it did happen. However, I admit I see my life as one big beautiful mess. Now I see this world from a different set of eyes. My illness taught me to be brave, to have courage when I need to, to have faith and pray. So, I do. The people I've met along my journey are people I'll never forget. My wonderful mother has taught me everything. She gave me all the tools for life. So, at 14 years old when I came down with a mental illness, believe it or not, I was pretty prepared to face this illness head-on. Still to this day I know how to advocate for myself because my beautiful mother was such a good advocate for me. When my mom (the earth angel) says something, she means it.

I had turned down going to a treatment facility in Vermont because I had Mainecare and Mainecare said no. My mom kept pushing for the retreat in Vermont. Things started changing when she told them she'd go to every newspaper, every radio station even the news channels. She would have to. Then their answer changed. When I was faced with my first psychotic break, I believe it was because I overdosed on pills in an attempt to kill myself. After that, I wound up staying in hospitals for 6 months and went to 3 different hospitals at that time too. I kept telling them I was better while being still completely delusional, and they discharged me. Then I'd snap out of it and go get help again. I finally let down my guard and said I need something more to help me.

 I need a guardian. So, to this day I have a guardian. I am not embarrassed or ashamed to tell people that I am proud of how far I've come in my life and all of the accomplishments I've made. You should be equally proud of your accomplishments. I live in a group home right now. I'm working on getting back on my feet after a failed marriage. I am so proud of the woman I've become. I'm kind, gentle, loving and do anything for anyone and that is how I know I will be okay. See if you carry good traits which everybody has then you can and will succeed. I've had mental health worker after mental health worker and I work best with the ones who have been there before. Not identical but those that I can relate to. So if you're struggling to connect with your provider find one you feel like you can relate to. I was a cheerleader in high school and while I have nothing against cheering, I should have played basketball. In the 8th grade felt was my first sign of depression. I felt it on such a deep level when I found out I didn't make the basketball team. I was devastated if only that teacher knew how badly I wanted that spot. But I left after I found out the bad news and, on my way, walking home from school, I got extremely depressed. I started thinking I'm not good enough I'll never be good enough. I'll leave school. Nobody knows how I feel. Don't tell anybody how I feel m so stupid. I'll stop trying. So what I did automatically was painted a smile on my face and went back to school the next day did everything I needed to do while feeling completely dead inside. I say dead because I wanted to feel nothing. So, I suppressed my feelings in order not to feel them. I became numb.

There's one song that I'd listen to, *Crawling* by Linkin Park that I could relate to 100 percent. So, when I hit sophomore year in high school everything hit me hard. I needed to get out of school and feel free from restrictions. So, I walked home from my high school and I swore I'd never return. My mom called the school and they put me in the Special Ed program I tried to stay there but I left after 2 weeks. Then I went to the alternative school. I left there too. That's when my mom sent me to the Brattleboro Retreat. What I found at the Brattleboro Retreat was peace of my mind, body, heart and soul. I felt by the world and I found a good place to cry. I cried and uplifted cried until I couldn't cry anymore. Then I felt at ease, at peace. I also talked a lot to the counselors there. And at night I'd pray to my angels. I'd talk to them and ask them for help. God never puts more on you than you can handle. I feel like I've been carrying the weight of the world on my shoulders so it's either he thinks I can handle it or I was put there by mistake. But I believe we write our own lives so guess I'm the one to blame. No wonder I beat myself up a lot. I've had a horrible past 3 years. I've had 2 failed suicide attempts and a hospitalization that lead me straight into a group home. After all that I had been through I wanted to live in a group home. So, I could take time to feel the earth beneath my feet again, and what I mean by that is so that

I can feel grounded again. I needed to find myself again. I needed to take care of myself again. In my last relationship, I forgot who I was. I needed to feel whole again, but at this point, it was bringing me to tears every day. If you're in a toxic relationship please get help. Right now, I'm taking my time finding the right person for me. I told myself I will not get serious with anyone until I feel it's right. Until they are that person. I had jumped in the past from relationship to relationship hoping they were the right one. They were not. I'm waiting for the right woman for me. My mother said something to me the other day that woke me up, as she always does. I love my mom. She's one amazing person. She said she knows some single girls my age but I have to get my life back on track before she introduces me. She's just giving me another nudge in the right direction. That's what I meant by my mother being an Earth Angel. She knows what to say and how to say it but no matter what she says I do it and it works. My father is that way too. He says it's always right.

I love both my parents so much. I couldn't ask for a better father or mother. There are many other people in my life like my mother and father. If they give you some advice you better listen. I've had many happy times in my childhood. My mom made sure of that. Christmas time she made sure the tree was packed with presents for my brother and me. And on Valentine's Day, she'd spend hours decorating Valentine's Day cards for us with chocolates. On Easter, my brother and I would run downstairs to see huge Easter baskets just for us. We always went to Fun Towns; we went to waterparks and York's Wildlife Kingdom. We also went to Storyland a lot. I was a very lucky child. I believe I struggle because I was sexually abused at age 6. I was brainwashed. He would buy me things because he was sexually abusing me. Being sexually abused does a lot of damage to your mind, body, heart and soul. I felt different most of my life. I felt like an outsider looking in on my family I am the black sheep. And nothing hurts more than that.

If you ask them, they will deny that but it's just how I feel. I've never been big on cutting my wrist or arms but I have beaten myself up every single day since childhood.

Chapter 4   No Justice

I'd tell myself I'm worthless daily. I've gotten better at that whereas I love myself now. I just really don't always like myself. I was sexually abused when I was six years old. This man that sexually abused me went 30 days in jail and got out early because of good behavior. But yet I have to suffer for the rest of my life because of what he did to me. Where's the justice in that? He's now off the sex offender's list because of some grandfather's law. When I say I've suffered because of this very evil man, I have suffered big time because of him. However, I refuse to be a victim anymore and be a survivor and start living. I can't let that have any control in my life anymore. I know in the end when he goes to die, he will get what is coming to him. There's a good book that I recommend called *The Courage to Heal* by Laura Davis. It's about becoming a woman survivor of child sexual abuse. I have picked myself up time after time - after each psychotic break. I have advocated for myself day after day.   I get this from my wonderful mother who helped me stand up for myself. So, I do.

Being a victim of sexual abuse is so painful. It caused such chaos in my life between my parents who were divorced. My father lived in New Hampshire and my mom lived in Maine and we would go see my dad every other weekend. Well, one day I was sitting on my couch at my mom's house and I was getting ready to eat an ice cream sandwich there was a loud knock at the door. Now my mom was a good mother, she was one of the best. She opened the door and a cop was there. My father had convinced a judge that my mom was unfit to raise us. Only because my dad said she was still in contact with the evil man that sexually abused me. My mom was not still in contact with him. My mom went to pack our things, bawling her eyes out. I'm crying; my brother is screaming and crying. The cops are looking around my mom's apartment and saying, "I'm so sorry mam, you are not an unfit mother. I'm sorry I have to do this. " My mom went to court to get us back and she was dressed in the most beautiful dress. When I saw her, I wanted to run up to her and give her the biggest hug and kiss and tell her I'm coming home soon, momma. Of course, my father knew my mom would win and the court gave us back to our mom. Both parents were trying to do the right thing. For me and my brother but when something like this happens it can tear families apart. I wish my mother knew how much I love her and how much I appreciate every little thing she has done for me and my brother as well.

It's difficult for me to go by the area where we used to live in where I was sexually abused. I've gone by there and it's hard for me to look at the porch. It's hard for me to look at the 104 on the door. Horrible things happened to me there. At times if I didn't do what he wanted me to do he'd whip off his belt and start hitting me with it. He'd become violent with me. Today I'm having a really bad day. It's painful to relive these painful memories. So ill break it up into sections about being a survivor of sexual abuse.

If you take a look outside at Mother Nature it may calm you down. It calms me. The fresh air, watching the wind blow and rustle the trees. I usually close my eyes and thank God for the gift to be silent in those moments. To be still in silence. It's a beautiful gift. When the world gets too much for me, I just close my eyes and picture all the weight leaving my body and I'm still. By still I mean quiet and calm, there's no movement spiritually within me. I'm getting rid of everything toxic and I'm letting everything go well. I could be at a heavy metal concert and still meditate and feel embraced by stillness. One thing I love to do is photography. I encourage you to practice meditation or let the weight leave your body as you're doing your favorite thing. You'll enjoy it so much more. Mind over matter. If you're depressed and are thinking about meditating, picture a beautiful rainbow surrounding your body. I remember a time when I first got sick and I wrote a suicide letter. I was just 14 years old and I ran from my house to Martins Point, a little water spot near my house. I stood there with a suicide letter in my hand and I didn't want anyone to find it. I just wanted it out in the universe before I killed myself. So, I dropped it in the water knowing that I was going to go home and take my life the next day. The next day came and I didn't kill myself. Then the days following I still didn't kill myself. Plus they were trying to get me into the Brattleboro Retreat, so how could I hurt myself without giving it a shot. If people only understood how I feel inside, they'd understand why I am how I am. I am beautiful, strong, kind, loving and a mess. All in the same breath. I find myself apologizing a lot for everything. I say *sorry* a lot. When I shouldn't have to. Like my father says to me *don't be.* He was right. I have an amazing father. He is pretty incredible. He is my best friend.

My father, my mother and my brother are the best things that have ever happened to me. My brother in his younger years was a troublemaker. If he wasn't getting in trouble with the police, he was getting in trouble at school. By the time he was 18 he enlisted in the army and he has turned out to be an incredible young man who recently got his degree. I am so proud of the handsome kind young gentleman he has become.

I never really knew my father's side of the family. I've always known my mother's side of the family. My doors are always open to both. From what I know from my father's side of the family is that they are down-to-earth, hard-, kind loyal people that love us with all their hearts. I love them too with all my heart. I don't see them often but when I do, I love it. They are all just as wonderful as the next. They have been very supportive of my mental illness. What I did to get myself through my hard times was that I wrote. I would journal. I'd listen to music when I was writing. It became a passion of mine. Then I wanted to help people through writing. Maybe if I told my story it could help someone else out. If I could just reach out to others and tell them you're not alone, that I've been there too. Maybe even just a little bit, it would help. Then it's worth writing a book. I used to say if I could just help one person through my pain, then everything I've gone through would be worth it.

I picture the day I die running into the light in this tunnel with my two dogs in front of me, their tails waving in the air, them jumping all around. God, don't I love them? When I got a divorce, I had to give one to the humane society and the other went with my ex-husband but I miss them and I love them. They are on my mind all the time every day. I pray that they are safe, happy and healthy.

I was bullied in the 8th grade by a girl who pretended she was my friend. She did it more discreetly. Then she said to me one day, "Do you know why I make fun of you so much? It's because I'm jealous of you." They talk behind my back, laugh at me, put me down. She'd make fun of my feet saying I had boat feet and big eyebrows. They'd laugh at me about the way I ate. They'd throw things at me until I got sick of it and left. When I left one day I left with a thump. I felt courageous. I was never going to talk to those bullies again and the truth is I have not ever since. Even if I didn't leave high school early I still would not have. They put me through hell. There were 3 of them. One of them I had known since the third grade, too. When I walked out of their house I felt so much better. You know when you take a stand and you walk out from an abusive situation you feel so good. You feel like the weight has been lifted. I promised myself I wouldn't let anyone walk all over me since then. I did nothing to her. In the end, I became a survivor of her bullying me. I started hanging out with a different crowd. These were the popular girls in high school. We became quick friends.

Freshman year in high school was going well, however, my mental illness was starting to manifest. I have to admit I had no clue what was happening to me. I was confused and lost. The only way I could describe it was *raw*. Everything felt so raw. What I mean by *raw* is that nothing was comfortable, everything was so miserable. There's this song that describes it perfectly. It's called *Crawling* by Linkin Park. That's what I mean by raw. It is only better with medications.

I have been on a lot of medications since age 14. I had behavioral issues and mental health issues. I do remember what it's like to be quote *normal* unquote. But if I could go back in time and chose to not get sick mentally I wouldn't. I'm happy now. Maybe not every day. But I found this peace inside of me that sustains me and grows with each passing breath. I would choose to be mentally ill and still see life through these lenses. I've gained so much more than I've lost. I've been this way most of my life. And although I may not always feel this way more often than not, I do. Mental illness is and can be a beautiful journey. Seeing life in your own unique way. Marching to your drummer and not letting anybody get you down for you being who you are. That was my biggest thing. What if my old friends made fun of me? I developed a thick skin from that. I didn't give a damn after all the years of old high school people saying I was a *snob* or a *bitch* and it would get back to me. The truth about me in high school was I had bipolar disorder and it wasn't being treated with medication yet. But having to understand and cope with it myself, then having to realize that teenagers don't always understand things like mental illness at that age was a pretty difficult thing to do. But once I got to the place I felt okay inside, I would find better friends down the road for me. I remember the day my mom

dropped me off at the Brattleboro retreat. I watched her leave and then there I was in Vermont, a new state, sitting in the chair all alone waiting for someone to come and get me. Trying to
ignore the fact that I didn't know a soul. So, I waited and finally, someone came to get me. I was terrified when I got to the unit. All the girls seemed so tough. They were from all parts of the USA. I was quiet and kind but uncomfortable. They soon put me on the well-behaved unit.

On t4 I met a man named Tom. The best man I have ever met in my life. He was a very wise old soul. Full of life and wisdom. I'm sure he wouldn't remember me now. It's been such a long time and he has seen so many people. But he changed my life. Every night after groups I'd write then sit in my chair in front of him and talk and talk. He'd give me the courage and strength to get from moment to moment. I owe this man my life. He saved me in so many ways. I'll never forget the last thing he said to me, "Nikita, you never cease to amaze me at your struggle to win the fight and you know I'm not supposed to have favorites but... well you get what I'm saying."
This man is a wonderful human being and to me is an Earth Angel too. So, my mom would come to see me every three months and it was when my mother's relationship with me wasn't at its greatest. She's an amazing mom. I was just a very troubled teen.

So of course, to me, everything was my mom's fault or somebody else's fault. I never really experimented with drugs or alcohol. I hated feeling out of control. People that were close to me during that time did and I'm happy to say they no longer do those horrible things to themselves. I had a boyfriend in high school who was such a sweetheart and I wish I could tell him why I was the way I was. I'm sure he may have figured out something. I can remember the first time I told my mom I might be gay. It took months to get the courage to tell her that I might be a lesbian and then I did one day, it came out. We were driving.
I said, "Mom?"
She said, "Yeah?"
I said, "I think I'm gay."
 She smiled and said, "Well, how do you know?"
I replied, "I'm not boy crazy like my friends and I get crushes on females."
She replied, "Ok, honey."
I didn't think she would give a negative response at all, to begin with, but I hadn't fully come to terms with it myself. I wanted to make sure that I had it right.

As I look back on my childhood, it was not a bad childhood, just bad things happened to me. My mother made sure we had everything we needed to survive, although I needed extra help. Now I'm 33 years old and living in a group home needing some help. I'm not judging myself but I'm happy that I am getting myself help and knowing enough to get the help I need. I am not someone who ignores the pain. I'm not too proud to get the help. Mental illness is truly the invisible disease. I've been treated badly by a lot of professionals who would call me manipulative. My goal was not to be manipulative; my goal was to advocate for myself. Those counselors don't matter anyway.

If you're telling a client off, take a look at yourself. These are the types of counselors we don't want to help us.

My father is a brilliant man who is kind, gentle and loving. He is my best friend. He recently had a couple of bad heart attacks and he survived. I love him and it's hard to see your loved one struggle. He's someone who has always been there for me, come hell or high water. I know death is a part of life but his heart attacks made me stop and think about what truly matters in life. My aunt Cindy, who is an Earth Angel, is dying. They gave her three years to live and she will be doing chemo every week for the rest of her life. She's a fighter she will hang in there until the very last second. She is a beautiful, loving courageous woman who has touched so many lives. The last time I heard she had made peace with the fact that she was going to die. She's been mostly preparing my mother for her dying. My mom and my aunt Cindy are best friends. My mom raised my aunt Cindy and her other siblings. Since my mom was older. My grandmother, my mom's mom, had schizophrenia so at just 5 years old, my mom was raising her siblings. I can't even imagine what my mom is going through. My aunt Cindy has always been my favorite aunt. When I was younger, I wanted to be just like her. She is a strong, confident - yet gentle woman whom I know will still be with us even after passing. I wish I had the right words as to how much she will be missed. I'll miss her tremendously.

Having a mental illness is not you. It's not even a part of you. It is what you struggle with but it does not define who you are as a human being. I cannot say that enough. I usually talk to my angels at night when things in my life become unbearable and are too much for me to handle. Sometimes I get a response. Depending on how my next day goes. If the next day is harder I know they are right there saying *Nikita you can handle this. You've got this. That's why it's harder today. Prove to yourself you can do this.* And I do. But some days I don't. I'd just rather sit there all day and not handle a thing. On those days I give up. I refuse to grow spiritually. I refuse to talk and get everything out. Those are my bad days. Which for the past 3 years I've had more often than not. I also talk to my angels about lessening the pain I feel every day. Usually mentally for me and emotionally. They usually do. I'll say too much is too much. With gentleness, they lift the pain and ease up on it. I talk to my angels about everything. Usually in my mind. I ask them for help and I usually get the help in one form or another. I hope when I die, I can talk to them in person and say kindly – *Was my life meant to so freaking hard? If it was then why? Because I would like to know what I was thinking when I signed up for this! And can you tell me exactly why I signed up for this? I'd appreciate that!*

Now when I was younger, I was a brat. However, a lot of bad things had happened to me so I was acting out. My mom was with someone abusive at the time so I'd act out more. I've literally been in therapy in one form or another my whole life and I still am. There's nothing wrong with that. I'd like to get myself to a place where I don't need therapy anymore. I wouldn't need a guardian id, have a full-time job, stand on my own two feet and not need anyone. Each day I'm getting closer to that goal. As I get older, I start to realize I could and can more than I had thought. The truth is I've felt alone for a very long time. Alone with everything I say and everything I do. When I was in a relationship I still felt alone and I'm looking for that person to complete me. I have a psychic friend that keeps saying *Nikita you will meet her take this time to love yourself more.* While I've heard that my entire life, I guess more work needs to be done before I find Mrs. Right. I don't know who she is yet or where she is but I love her. I was told I would meet her soon. And I'm praying that I do. I would do anything to meet Mrs. Right.

I have a lot of doubts. Am I not good enough? Am I going to sabotage my relationships with people without meaning to? I was brainwashed when I was sexually abused and ever since then, I haven't felt good enough. I haven't even felt good enough to wear makeup in fear lately that everyone would laugh at me. Not feeling worthy is such a hard thing to deal with. You feel like everything and everyone is superior to you and you're just the little man on the totem pole. It's such a strange feeling. I've gone years without really making eye contact with anyone because I felt unworthy. Having self-worth issues has nearly dictated my whole life. I think through this book and I pray that you do it with me or even just think about it. We reclaim our self-worth back. I've spent my whole life pretty much feeling unworthy. Unworthy of what? Of *everything*. Even a gift. If I could tell survivors of sexual abuse one thing it would be this. You are worthy. It's true. I'm worthy. You are worthy.

Sometimes things cut so deep we don't know how to get rid of the pain so we either lash out at others or cut ourselves or go to any lengths or extremes to get rid of the pain. I got into an abusive relationship that lasted a very long time. It wasn't one's fault or the other, it was both of us together. We were just toxic together. We had a house full of animals and all of that was too much stress on me. But what I had learned was that there's no need to settle. If you're in a relationship where you're unhappy don't stay because even if you end up being alone you can search for what you want not just with a relationship but with your whole life. I've gone on dates but not one of them would be her. The right one for me. There's that song by Melissa Etheridge. *I want to be in love.* It's true, I do but only for Mrs. Right this time. I've been single for three years now and it's been a little lonesome but peaceful and it's given me time to work on myself. I told myself I'd do things the right way and work on myself before jumping into the next relationship. I wish I could meet my person but I know the universe works in mysterious ways. She's out there waiting for me too. At the end of my past relationship, he wanted a fight. I didn't give him one. I wanted a civil divorce and it was. It was nice. I talked to a psychic she had said I'd meet my person before the year 2020 is done. I hope she's right. I have my mom telling me she knows people that would be a good match for me but I've got to get my life back on track. Which is true. I do and I have been doing that and still am. It takes a long time for me to soul search. I take every opportunity I can. Whether it be fifteen minutes or ten years. Take some time for yourself. There's nothing more special than that. You matter. In my past relationship I thought I was doing right but deep down you know you're doing nothing right if you're not right for that person.

My favorite persons in this whole world are my mother and my father. I find my mom and her sense of humor hilarious. She's one woman I wouldn't want to piss off though. My dad is my best friend. I guess you could say they are both my two favorite people. They both come in first place. But my all-time favorite person who has the most beautiful soul is mother Teresa. I love her writing.

Angels everywhere I used to pray to them for everything to get better. They always answered as I mentioned before even if they didn't. My father used to be a private investigator and I used to go to work with him sometimes when he was working. I thought that was the coolest job. I had to be very quiet and still while he videotaped someone lifting a heavy object when they weren't supposed to be. It was exciting however I could never do that for work. I thought then I love to have a job like that and be like dad but that job is kind of dangerous. You never know if that person your filming is going to come after you or not.

However, I thought it was a lot of fun. I had to sit very still and low down in the car. My father would never take me on anything too dangerous though. He'd have to know for a fact I'd have to be completely safe. When my dad lived in New Hampshire we had a huge brown house. It was huge and nice with a big trampoline in the front yard. We would jump on that thing until we couldn't jump anymore or until we got called in for dinner. My father was married at the time to a beautiful woman named Sally. When they fought, everyone knew to stay away. Sally recently passed away. She was caught up in a love triangle and was shot. I'll never forget my last talk with Sally or the last hug. I miss her. I was unable to attend her service because I was delusional but I know if she knew how sick I was she would understand. Anyways the way things were at my mom's was so different from my dad's. They were like 2 different worlds. But that was the way life had to be. I wish honestly, they didn't live so far apart and that they had taken the time to work out their differences for their children if not for anything else. That was the most painful part. You feel like it's your fault. When it's not. You have a parent who is blaming the other parent for everything that's gone wrong and vice versa, that is not healthy for your children. They get along great now but back then they never did. Unfortunately. But out of everything for the most part they did try their hardest to keep it away from us. We just had parents that loved us so much they just didn't see things the same way. There was no harm done. Just a lot of bickering.

When I was younger, I was placed in a beauty pageant and I got up there and said everything I was supposed to say. It was at the local mall. I ended up winning but they called someone else's name but my number. Well, they couldn't take it back so she got the crown. Now my mother still thinks to this day that I was screaming and crying when we left because I didn't get my crown. That wasn't true. What's true is I saw the other girls screaming and crying and I thought that was what you were supposed to do when you lost in the pageant. Other than that, it didn't bother me. My mom was *like OMG! No more beauty pageants for you again. Take it gracefully little girl, take it like a champ.* Either way, you look at it - whether I wanted to cry or not I didn't take it like a champ or gracefully. I think I was trying to figure out why the other girl was crying so I guess I thought it was the right thing to do to make you cry. My mom did not think it was fun at all. She said no more beauty pageants for you. She also told me this funny story of when I was younger and I got a papercut on my finger and all day i had my finger up in the air and not once did I put that finger down. Even when I had to go to the bathroom, I had my finger up in the air, which is why still to this day people tell me I have hypochondria. I do. I used to call it *hypocondamaniac.*

I started going to college around age 22. Around that time, I was so unhappy with my life. I wasn't where I wanted to be. I was in an unhealthy relationship. I just wanted to be alone. I needed to figure things out for myself. Writing got me through it. If it wasn't for writing I probably would have attempted suicide. They are telling me now that I have *schizoaffective disorder* which is pretty much bipolar disorder with psychotic features. I've gone to see counselor after counselor and med manager after ed manager. I've had case manager after case manager and I still don't feel quite ready to make it on my own. This is why I'm here in this group home today. I am never ashamed to say I need this kind of help from anybody. If I need it I am going to utilize it until I feel I'm ready for the next step. I'm proud of myself. I have come so far in my life with all that has happened to me.
I have been sexually abused.
I've been abused by two of my mom's partners.
At age 14 I had been put on heavy-duty medication.
I've been bullied.
I've gone through a lot. To this day I am doing so much better. I'm proud of myself. I go through paranoia, delusional thinking,

psychotic breaks, depression, panic attacks, anxiety and hallucinations. That's a lot to deal with daily then you've got the daily stuff that you have to take care of. That is why I've been so hesitant about getting a job. All of those things I listed get to be way too much for me most days and I hate it when people try to push me to do something I'm not ready for.

Chapter 6   Voices

In my last relationship, I was pushed to do things I was not ready to do and I started having breaks. Too much stress, little sleep, high anxiety all the time. I needed a nice calming relaxing environment. It was not. I started seeing things and becoming delusional. I'd forget sometimes who I was or where I was. I'd give people a different name. I was up all hours of the night laughing out loud to the voices in my head or myself. I thought I was talking to people and didn't recognize it as just voices in my head. I had recently been praying to Archangel Raphael about dying and letting me go to heaven as I usually do. Well, this past week I had a scare, I got up the other day at 5:00 am and I couldn't breathe. I went downstairs in a panic. The staff here said it was a panic attack. I'd stand up and my oxygen level would drop and my pulse would rise. The nurse here came in and called an ambulance. She thought it might be blood clots in my lungs. Sure enough, they did some tests and found blood clots. They think it was caused by smoking while I took the birth control pills.

Now I know all the times I said I wanted to die, I came to terms in the hospital that I didn't. I just wanted to live more. So I'm going to try that. They then checked my legs and it turned out my left leg had blood clots in it too. That whole time death was staring me in the face and I was staring back. At that point I didn't want to die anymore, I was terrified. I realized I wanted to live. It was so hard to sit there in the ICU and not have anyone there sitting with you (because of the coronavirus), only one person could visit for one hour. Then getting woken up at 3:00 am by them taking a wire out of my neck. It was so difficult not to cry. I was terrified the whole time. I could have died. I had so many blood clots on my lungs and my left leg. It's been a week and a half and I'm still trying to recover. All of that from smoking and taking birth control pills. I can say now it's been 2 weeks and three days since I've had a cigarette. It's almost like Raphael was saying - *Ok, Nikita you're right at death's door, make your choice. This time is now. I've listened to you for years saying you wanted to die.*

I quickly said I want to live. I'm scared. My mom would miss me, my dad would struggle so much with my death. My brother would too. I want to live. I am so sorry for saying I wanted to die. I have the nurse at Community Health and Counseling Services in Bangor to thank. She's the one that sent me to the hospital and kept pushing it. She said there might be blood clots in your lungs. Sure enough, there were. All I could say was I was so sorry that I had wanted to die. When death is staring you in the face it's different. Now I am on blood thinners and while I was there, I had good people stopping by to see me. I'm feeling better now and doing this while quitting smoking has been hard but I am getting better with the smoking piece. They moved me around a couple of times from the ICU to the regular units, back to the ICU again. So that is my brush with death. I realized I had so much to live for and I hope and pray that if you ever think about ending your life, don't do it. Please don't. You are loved, you will be missed even if you feel like that's not true. It is true it's scary when you're knocking on death's door. I picture this life as a school, the ultimate college and we come here to learn. Then once we are finished here, we go back home. I certainly can't wait to go home but I know I have so much work I need to get done here. Now granted, I'm starting now at 33 years old but I have to start somewhere. I'm going to start by writing books and working. These are things I should have done earlier in my life but now's as good of a time as any. I feel like I've struggled so much in my life and have not had time for fun while people my age are out having fun. I was at home depressed thinking of ways to end my life. I miss those days where I did have fun beginning high school, loved us and things just kept changing so fast. Next thing I knew I was in psychiatric wards time after time again. I understood why my mom took every avenue that she took with me. She told me the truth about everything. She never sugarcoated anything for me. She has told me what was real and what was not real. and by doing this she wants me to stay in reality for the most part. I owe a lot to my mom for being that real with me. When I had my first break down at 22 years old, my mom had no clue where I was. She had been trying to find me for a while and she got my call and brought me to Saint Mary's Hospital to be evaluated. If I could just say from my heart what it's like to go through a psychotic break and have nobody there by your side because that's what usually was like for me. Because if I'm sick I have no way of calling them to let them know that I'm not okay. No way to tell them I need help. I remember one time when I was driving one of our cars that was not good in the snow and it was snowing out. I must have had a guardian angel with me because it would have been a big wreck. I don't wish that pain upon anyone. I am constantly wondering why I took on this life in this world. I wonder what I'm here to learn and I wonder what I'm here to be taught. Sometimes I feel like nobody else knows my pain. Sometimes I feel like I'm the only one that knows my pain and that may be true but it leaves me feeling alone and isolated. I guess it is why I am writing this book. I want to share my life with you in hopes that you will feel better about your situations and life. Know that you are not alone. All I want to do is help people through my pain and that little place in my life where I want to get my stuff together. I'm trying to get my way off of disability. I want to write books I want to get a full-time job. I want to pay rent on my own and do everything on my own for once in my life.

The other day my mom talked to me. My mom had never said anything to me about how to get my life together. She asked me now. I replied that I have my life together and doing this and I'm doing that. But I knew the truth, I've been too scared to know how to get my life together. For the past four or five years of my life, my life has been about psychotic breaks. I've had one break down after another and it would not. Maybe it's the stress of living in this group home or stress that I had to deal with in my past relationship. There could have been other things too.

Psychotic breaks are scary - terrifying. Let me tell you about one time when I had a full psychotic break. I was 22 years old I was living with my partner at that time and I don't know if I took something to try and kill myself or if it just happened on its own. I did have a huge psychotic break. I don't know who I was or where I was. All I remember is a fight about the cats that we had. All I remember is that there's a huge fight between my partner and me at the time. I sat down on my couch and everything went black and when I woke up everything that had been black wasn't black anymore. It wasn't a different world, but I was having delusions that my partner, and at times my parents, were trying to kill me. So they were walking up and down the street dressed in black because they didn't want to be seen. Next thing you know they're scratching on my screen. They made their way into my apartment somehow and are whispering things in my ears. I heard a gun right behind my head and I thought they're about to pull the trigger. They told whispered in my ear that they were going to kill me. There were black trash bags all over my apartment- on the floor, on the walls and the ceilings. They told me that this prevented a mess when the gun fired. There wouldn't be a way to find out who did it. Throughout my breakdowns, I've learned a lot about myself, about the world, about people, about kindness, about compassion, about true love for myself and others. I'm not a professional. I'm someone who has lived this life, Just someone who can only tell you what I've been through. I hope it helps you through your life. I learned a lot about nature. I've learned a lot about fear. Most of all, that "good" removes fear so it can help you to grow. You can turn something negative into a positive. Love is all there is. If we just took the time each day to do something nice for somebody else, whether it's giving up your spot in line at the grocery store to someone else who may need it more than you. Or letting someone go in line in front of you while you're driving. Or whether you see someone in the grocery store who has had a bad day, and it looks like they've had a very bad day - you smile, at them, maybe that would brighten up their whole day. When I say, "Love is over, that it is for me." Nothing else matters, you matter to me, people matter to me and I matter to me. But the number one thing in this world that matters the most is love. Love truly is all there is.

I stop and look back at some of my actions, I say why would I do or say that. My actions weren't kind or nice, that wasn't a polite or compassionate response. I forget again but I truly believe if love is all there is then I better start showing it. I think sometimes you can get so mixed up with the world and the chaos and then drama you forget the important things in life like love. You forget about loving one another, being there for one another, and helping someone. Another thing lately is I've been so angry about my mental illness I just can't seem to get it through my head that there is someone who will love me as I love her. I'm going to not give up. I've tried those online dating sites; every date that I've had so far seems not to work. It's my illness it scares them away, I think, but I could be wrong.

Since my past relationship I've done a lot of thinking about what I want in a relationship and what I was searching online for a relationship. I realized that people like that are not what I want either. Some of them actually came and told me that it wasn't the mental illness piece they didn't want. I mean they didn't come out and say it but they said it in other ways. My life has been beautiful despite whether I'm struggling or not. I wouldn't trade my life for the world. Even when I'm thinking about suicide, I wanted to kill myself.

Everything is a learning lesson. I thank God for the lessons learned in life and thank God for my family who I absolutely love. I'm praying for my aunt Cindy who is such an Earth Angel. She has cancer and is still going through chemo once every week. She is one remarkable woman. She's beautiful, strong independent, loving, compassionate, and kind. She's everything good and I love her more than words can say. She is so spiritually open and fun-loving. We are all having a hard time with this but I know I should be around her all the time. I love her very much. When I was younger, I would go to her house, we used to pick strawberries from her strawberry patches. I used to pick blueberries that were in her blueberry bushes. I have been so lucky to have her as my aunt. Blessed to have her as a part of my life.

I believe in angels. I believe in Earth Angels. I believe in Spirit guides. I believe in a higher power. I believe in Mother Nature. I believe in Jesus. I believe in love most of all. I believe that your angels and spirit guides are always with you. I believe that you are never alone coming into this world. I believe that we came here to learn. I believe when we die we go back home to heaven which is our true home. I believe in soulmates. I believe someone may or may not find their soulmate on Earth. I know I've been looking for my soulmate. The psychic is telling me I'll meet her by the end of 2020. Well, I hope that's true. I do because I've been searching everywhere for my soulmate. If there is one thing I want in this world it is my soulmate. You could offer me billions of dollars and I'd still just want my soulmate. Hopefully my next book I'll be able to write about how I found my soulmate.

My high school years were the tipping point in my life. When I started high school, I was bipolar and unmedicated. I needed a lot of medication and a lot of therapy. So much was going on inside of me. I had a lot of energy from being manic. At home, I felt depressed but nobody saw the depressed side of me. I didn't share it with anybody. Then one day I went over to one of my friends' houses and I just started crying and crying and crying until I couldn't cry anymore. Now when you're in high school it looks really bad when you're sitting there crying for no reason at all. My friend instantly didn't want to be my friend anymore because it wasn't the cool thing to do. I went home and cried some more. They try picking me up after church and it looks like I just cried the whole time. I just kept crying.

I laid there in bed for about 6 months only getting up to eat or go to the bathroom and that was it. During that time, I lost all my friends because at that age you don't understand mental illness like an adult does. It is seen as weird or strange to make fun of you, calling you names as I'm assuming my old friends did to me. So not only did I have to deal with this situation, I had to deal with tons of medication that made me gain a bunch of weight. Add to this, huge braces on my teeth. My mom insisted that I get braces and they did straighten my teeth nicely, but I was not a popular girl anymore. I loved school but I stayed at home and tried not to have a care in the world anymore. I tried to ignore everything that was going on at school about me, all the rumors about me, and then about the time that I went to the Brattleboro Retreat. I started to feel a little more at ease – that maybe the rumors about me had stopped at my old high school. I would never choose friends like that for myself again. Later on in life, I met some good friends. Come to think about it, I was miserable in high school. Everything had to be a certain way, you had to be a certain way. Everybody wanting you to dress a certain way. Act a certain way, wear your hair a certain way, have your nails done a certain way, and wear your clothes a certain way. I felt you had to be exactly who they wanted you to be at all times. They want you to skip doing homework. If your friends wanted you to stay in the hallways and gossip, you would stay out in the hallways and gossip, because that's a cool thing to do. If they thought anythi8ng was a cool thing to do - you better do it. That's what it was like for me in high school. If you didn't commit to the role that they wanted you to be, you'd get kicked out of the group. Basically, just be who they want you to be.

"Nooooooooo! not anymore," voices were telling me!

I grew up in a small town in Maine. Everybody knew everybody's business. That was always hard for me. I would have loved to have grown up in New York City or Chicago. I'm more of a city girl than a country girl. Don't get me wrong I love the country. My grandfather had a farm I used to love to go there and pig scramble. We used to love to try and lasso the bulls. But as I got older, I realized the city fits me best. I'd love to live in New York City.

My life has been chaotic. It's been hard, stressful and very painful. I don't expect sympathy from anybody, I don't want it. What I want is to be able to help people. I remember one time

I sat on my grandmother's bathroom floor and had a razor in my hand and I was thinking about suicide. it took me a good hour or so to talk myself back out of it. I thought about my grandmother and how she would feel. What about my mother and how she would feel? What about my aunt and how she would feel? I thought about life in general. Life is beautiful. The opportunity to learn from life, that's it's a beautiful gift given to us. Committing suicide will take that away from us. Life may seem very difficult sometimes but if you look at the pros and the cons – you will see there are more pros than cons.

I've been in situations where I felt like people were following me with cameras, so I ended up walking around in the emergency room in my robe looking as unstable as can be. I was walking around a lot, around the chair in my room over and over again. They were putting me on the news. They were following me everywhere. I went even outside; I felt like the whole world was watching me. I also felt like the staff could come in and do whatever they wanted to me, including killing me on the news.   Over the entire state of Maine, everybody was watching the news of me in my room. Then I was sent to Spring Harbor. Spring Harbor Hospital is a 100-bed free-standing nonprofit psychiatric hospital located in Westbrook, Maine. It is one of two free-standing psychiatric hospitals in the state of Maine and offers services for both children and adults. felt the same way, like everybody was lined up in the hallways watching me. People that I knew before and others that I didn't know, they're saying horrible things about me. They were following me into my room. I was hearing voices and seeing things that were not there. Smelling things that aren't there. I was terrified that my Mom hated me. I thought my father hated me and my brother hated me. My entire family on both sides hated me. It is a scary thing to go through. I thought it was "Spring Hardware" and that everybody there, clients and patients were putting signs all over me. They were writing stuff all over me. I felt like the cook didn't even like me. I thought that everything that I heard in my head was saying horrible things to me. Hearing voices is terrifying. Some people out there choose to live that way.

Another period in my life when I had a full-blown psychotic break, I was choosing to stay that way too. The medication that I was taking at a hospital sent me back out of the delusions. I chose to stay in reality and sometimes I wish that the mental health professional workers knew what it was like to be in our shoes for a while because I run into too many counselors lately that do not care. That's in my opinion.

 Well, when I had blood clots in my lungs and blood clots in my left leg, I finally got the rest and relation I needed to do and haven't done it a long time. When I was younger, I watched the waves crashing down at the beach. There's nothing more healing to me than that. I used to love finding sea glass. And finding other things at the beach.

When I was younger, my mother had an abusive partner. You should tell me what to wear to school and it was at that time I wanted to be cool by wearing wide-leg jeans. My friends used to sneak jeans in for me to wear - the cool ones. Sometimes we went up to a bathroom in City Hall to change. I was hoping that someone would catch me coming out of City Hall. Most times I just changed at school though. My mom's partner said I couldn't wear makeup. She controlled everything we did – down to the last piece of toilet paper. I think my mom was afraid to leave her for so long and this person was extremely abusive to her. My mom was miserable with her and we were all miserable with her there in our household. She was mean and abusive and she didn't let anybody else see her true side; it was all behind closed doors. My brother and I went through a lot as children. But we also had a lot of fun too. My brother and I used to watch Monday Night Raw Wrestling. We used to wrestle with each other. We had so much fun. I love my brother; he is the best big brother.

My mental illness is not myself - it's not me – it's something that I struggle with. I have story after story of things that I've dealt with regarding my mental illness. I've had psychotic break after psychotic break. I have no shame in saying that. If it's one thing I've learned in my life, *be who you are and don't hold back. Love who you are - no matter what anybody says.* The psychotic breaks that I was having were so terrifying. In between psychotic breaks, I am terrified that it was going to happen again. Just trying to get myself help before another psychotic break started. I would call the Maine Mental Health Crisis Hot Line. Some of the crisis workers were not that nice to me. So,they would turn me down for help. Professionals in the field think it's okay to treat clients with disrespect but is not okay. Some of the crisis workers do treat clients with respect, they're amazing people. I find there is more good staff than bad staff, which is good.

When I was sexually abused the whole world came crashing down around me. It felt like it was my fault. It felt like my mother was suffering because of me and it felt like my brother was suffering. Victims of sexual abuse need to know they are okay. They need to know they are safe and are going to be okay. I was put in therapy immediately and ever since I haven't stopped going to therapy. That evil man did a lot of damage to me. It damages your mind, it damages your heart, your body and your soul. You spend a lot of years searching for those pieces of you that you lost or that you feel like you've lost. It takes time to build up your self-esteem again and it also takes a lot of time to tell yourself and believe it - that you are worthy. You are worthy. You're just as worthy as anybody else. My father was the one that I disclosed to. my stepmom at the time had seen the signs that I was being sexually abused so my father asked me if anything was happening to me. I finally broke down and said yes. When something like this happens to you, you're scared to tell anybody. Now this man – this evil man was supposed to stay out of the town that I lived in he actually moved into that town. He got less than 30 days in jail and got grandfathered off the sex offender list. Where is the Justice in that? The one thing that makes it better is that I know when he dies he's not going to a very good place. He will get what he deserves afterlife.

There are good books out there (Bass & Davis, The Courage to Heal) about healing if you're a victim of sexual abuse. I spent a lot of years working hard at getting over what he did to m and getting past all the pain that he put me through and put my family through. My mother and I had come through hard times. As I write this book I feel like I am starting to heal more and more. I hope it can help you to heal also.

Once I divorced my ex, I had to get rid of my dog. Her name was Shines and I like to think that when my day comes to leave this earth, she will be right there in the tunnel of light waiting for me. There are a lot of things I've lost during my divorce but I miss her most. I love her. When I went to leave to go stay at my mom's as I was leaving my ex's, Shine put her face on mine telling me, "It's okay to go, mom. I understand." It was so hard to walk out that door without my dog but I know I had to do it. I've had to drive by the old apartment so many times. I hated driving down that street.

I want to talk about how so many of us feel. we are not our disorder. I know I've said that a couple of times before we can be successful at anything, we want to be successful. All of our dreams can come true. Never let anyone tell you differently. You could be anything you want in this whole world. You can be successful at anything. There are lawyers and doctors out there with mental health issues. There are movie stars with a mental health diagnosis. There are so many successful people with mental health issues. If you set your mind to it, you can be whoever you want to be in this world. Don't let what anybody says hold you back. People say things out of jealousy or to frighten someone. Just don't ever let anybody tell you, you can't do something because you have mental health diagnosis, because you can. There's so much more to you than your mental illness, I cannot stress that enough.

Chapter 8   Loving Yourself

From this moment on I'm going to vow to love myself more. I've done everything cruel to myself in the past intentionally. And because of never loving myself enough I wasn't assertive to deal with bulimia. I've overdosed several times to try and kill myself and all because I told myself I was no good - not worth it. I beat myself up to the max. I wish I could go back in time and talk to myself then and say, "It's okay not to listen to criticism and to be who you are – despite what anyone has to say."

I look back in time and I see myself as a sad girl who lost friends. A sad girl who lost part of herself to big dreams she didn't even know what they were yet. Now I know. I want to help people through the examples of my pain. If I can help just one person it would make all my pain worth it. I used to think if one person knew exactly what I was going through while living it just like me then somebody out there would know how to help me. That's not possible. This disease is an invisible disease. Mental illness is not like a broken leg or broken arm where you can see it. It is an Invisible disease where you can tell someone your symptoms.

So, today when I start loving myself, I want to think about all the changes necessary. First, start by telling myself in my mind I'm good enough. If I have negative thoughts in my mind about myself then I will replace them with positive thoughts. I want to start talking to angels more. I want to meditate more. Every day when I wake up in the morning I will come up with new goals. I always say I will not change my life even if I could. However, I don't know about psychotic breaks. Is the pain worth no gain? If I can help people with having gone to them That would make it worth it. it seemed to me that^^^^^^^^^^

It seemed to me that no matter who I reached out to at that time, they did not understand what I was going through. I told provider after provider. Most really didn't have a clue what I was going through. At least I felt that way. It takes a strong person to have psychotic breaks and help themselves struggle the whole way through it. Not only did I become stronger, I also started believing in myself more. There's always that fear that the psychotic breaks will come. While I'm here at this group home, I'm going to get all the tools necessary to make sure that there is less of a chance of them happening again. Recently, I was delusional and going through a divorce. My ex and I were meeting at the lawyer's office and it was pouring rain outside. So I thought I'd go dancing out in the rain and I did. I would say it's so calm and peaceful at the time but it looked completely unstable. It was helping me cope with what was going on in my life. Now I go out and dance in the rain if I feel an episode coming on? No, but during my break downs I was always doing stuff like that. I wish I could say I had a lot of support during that time in my life but I did not. I had a lot of counselors trying to helping me but personally, in my life, I did not have much help. I relied on my counselors the most. What am I doing to love myself nowadays? I'm taking time for myself each day whether it is writing, listening to my favorite music or meditating. Struggling with bipolar disorder is a difficult way to live. You see things with just such a different lens. I started getting sick around age 14 and while I was struggling, I took everything in. I went from being an extrovert to an introvert pretty quickly. I wanted to take everything in. I became sad and felt alone however being quiet, keeping to myself to try to heal my pain. When I was closed off from the world and I did my own thing I felt almost healed knowing that I was taking time for myself. That was all that mattered at that moment. I've done some pretty outrageous things having psychotic breaks but the main thing that I learned throughout my psychotic breaks is that I do love myself and get help. Even if I had to walk to the hospital, I I still got myself help. There were those days I did have to walk to the hospital completely delusional on my own having to check myself in. I want to explain to everybody there - even the crisis workers there - why I was there and I was completely delusional at those times. Sometimes you don't even know who you are. Sometimes it's like you're living in a whole new world. That world might be terrifying and at other times it could be happy. Once it starts to get worse and you start questioning if it's real or not - then I know to get the help. The first psychotic break that I have had was when I was discharged from one of the hospitals; I made it home to my phone to call my mom. So she came to pick me up to bring me back to the hospital and into the emergency room. We were waiting there and I thought I was having an exorcism done on myself because I thought I was possessed. So my arms and feet were flying in the air. Singing out I things. My mom just held my hand and told me everything will be okay. So, after my waiting room exorcism, they took me back into the hospital so they could evaluate me. I never felt so laughed at in my life. Some of these professionals were laughing at me.

This past Christmas I spent at the group home and I did a lot of thinking about all the Christmases that I had spent alone usually when I was delusional. I thought about everything and wondered how my dog was doing. I prayed that somebody nice adopted her from the animal shelter. I thought about my family and how they're spending it together and how they invited me each Christmas and I kept saying no because I was sick and I didn't want them to see me like that. My mother has this way of snapping back into reality. Even if I'm not having a breakdown, she's blunt and all In the same breath she's kind and gentle and lets you know that she cares.

I had a psychic one time tell me I was an Earth Angel. immediately thought of my grandmother Jeanette, my mother Lynn, and my aunt Cindy, they are the Earth Angels. Although my grandma Jeanette passed away, I'm sure she is in heaven and is an angel up in heaven. My Grandma Jeanette had faced hard times in her life struggling herself with a mental health diagnosis. She was inspiring. She had struggled so much and got herself healthy again. I am and was so proud of her. I'm proud that my aunt was going through a very hard time right now. My mom is also going through a very hard time right now. I'm so proud of them; they are two beautiful souls that can make it through anything. This world is beautiful. We come into this world I believe knowing what we are going to do here, what we have come here for and everything is set in place in grade school, high school, and the rest of your life you can have other ways to learn your destiny, it doesn't always have to be school. We are here to fulfill a role in our society to make this society a whole. Then once we die, we give all our learned information to each other and our higher power.

Exercise 1 Love & Fear

The more fear we face the more knowledge we get. There's so much to learn from fear. Ask yourself what are the things you feared the most? This earth has tons of things to fear on it. I was afraid of bats, but I just found out that they are extremely gentle - so my fear went away. Learn from fear. Fear will teach you everything you need to know about yourself.

Take a pen or pencil and write down all the things you love about yourself on these pages.

NOTES

2. Think of all the things in your life that made you happy –
write them.

Exercise 2.

Take the next ages to talk about fear and pain:

1. What is your biggest fear?

2. Why is this your biggest fear?

3. What is stopping you from facing this fear head-on every day?

4. Does this fear cause you pain?

Write over the next few pages about your biggest fear and
how it causes you pain.

Okay after each exercise ask yourself *How do I feel?*

I know I usually feel better after reading and getting that all out. I usually write about my fears and find ways that I can get past those fears.

Dear Reader:

As I end this book, I want to say thank you. Thank you for reading my book. Thank you for walking down this journey with me. I am blessed to have written this book for you. I would also like to talk about mental illness. I didn't make any connection to my spirituality when I first became ill - bipolar disorder. At first, I felt there nothing else that could grab on to my life. Then, I found spirituality. I started praying and became more of an introvert. I started talking to my angels. I found peace. What it was like to be still in the -silence - not to have a single thought and just be in the moment. I feared the silence so much. I learned eventually that I was walking down a different path, one that I never knew existed. My life has changed drastically and now when I look back, I don't want that old road that I thought I was going to go down, that road to me seemed more superficial and shallow. I wanted a more challenging road. And that's what I got. Please take care of yourself even if you feel like you have nobody there to help you. You have to love yourself through the whole process and love who you are. Fear can be a pretty powerful thing. but it will not control you unless you let it. Overall I am a strong loving, kind, courageous, sweet and amazing – a person just like everybody else is. That is what I learned from writing this book. I thank you for walking down this road with me and I look forward to writing more books soon. Just remember you are worth it, you are strong, capable, loving, sincere and you can live all of your dreams. **All of your dreams can come true. No matter what your dream is, it can come true.**

I'm going to leave the next few pages as notes that you can write on about what you learned from this book. Similar to a journal, to process what you might have gone through while reading this book. If it was painful because you were abused too or if you've had a similar psychotic break. If it brought up a lot of stuff about your psychotic break. So please take the next few pages to write about whatever is there needing to be set free.

God bless you.

Nikita Wing